St Teresa's
WAY OF PERFECTION
for everyone

# St Teresa's
# WAY OF PERFECTION
## for everyone

**Elizabeth Ruth Obbard**

**New City**

First published in 2002
in Great Britain by
New City
Unit 1, Polaris Centre
41 Brownfields
Welwyn Garden City
Herts, AL7 1AN

© 2002 Elizabeth Ruth Obbard

2nd print 2016

Cover design by Tomeu Mayans

British Cataloguing in Publication Data:
A catalogue reference for this book is available
from the British Library

ISBN 978-0-904287-78-3

Typeset in Great Britain by New City

Printed and bound in Malta by
Gutenberg Press Ltd

# Contents

*For the Aylesford 'Tuesday Group'*

# INTRODUCTION

*The Way of Perfection* was first written around 1566 for young sisters belonging to the convent Teresa of Avila had recently founded in her native city.

Teresa, one of the Church's acknowledged teachers of prayer, founded this convent dedicated to St Joseph after a deep conversion experience in middle age. Most of her youth had been spent in the struggle to live a spiritual life, while being dogged with difficulties attendant upon her outgoing temperament and desire to please others. Eventually she was granted the grace she sought. Praying one day before an image of the wounded Christ her heart was touched and she resolved to follow her Lord in total faithfulness.

In the course of re-evaluating the religious life she was already living as a nun, Teresa determined to return to the original inspiration of the Carmelite Order and interpret its hermit beginnings in a way suited to women living in community in sixteenth century Spain. For this enterprise she gathered together a small group of novices and set about inaugurating a lifestyle focused exclusively on prayer.

Teresa, a relational person through and through, saw prayer as being the life blood of growing intimacy with God. It was prayer that would be the first duty of her sisters; so when the young women who came

to join her asked her to teach them how to pray, Teresa acceded to their request with a little book called *The Way of Perfection.*

In what she wrote Teresa wanted to make clear that praying was inseparable from a whole way of life and was not just about 'saying prayers'; hence she devoted the first part of the work to some basic principles of Christian living. Only then did she embark on more specific teaching about prayer, which she modelled on our Lord's own prayer, the *Our Father.*

Teresa had 'beginners' in mind as she wrote; people who wanted to pray and were just starting to do so seriously. She offers practical advice for living and praying. And she does so with gentle humour, and with knowledge of, and compassion for, human weakness. Nevertheless, she does not hide the fact that to live and to pray are so intertwined that we cannot divorce them from one another. We pray as we live; we live as we pray.

This book will give you some insight into Teresa's teaching as set forth in *The Way of Perfection.* It comes as an invitation to all people, whatever their age, whatever their stage of development. Teresa insists that anyone can pray if they want to pray. Anyone can love God in their life if they want to love him. It may be a gradual process, but a life of friendship with God awaits you, through a growing friendship with the Lord in prayer, and a growing friendship with those among whom you live your daily life.

Of course, this book as it stands is only an introduction to Teresa's teaching, it is the most basic of her works and in some ways the most personal. I have wanted to make it relevant to all, not just to the nuns Teresa originally wrote for.

Human nature is a constant wherever we are. Anyone can recognise themselves in these pages. To no one is the way of prayer barred. All we have to do is to want the Lord, being 'determined with a strong determination' to live for him and to have him as our friend and companion day by day.

Teresa writes as she speaks: directly, familiarly, and not always logically! It is this style I have tried to preserve, so that Teresa actually communicates personally with each of her present readers, just as she did so many years ago when she gathered her young sisters around her and began to teach them about the path that leads eventually to union with God. It is that path, taking us on the journey of prayer, which she terms *The Way of Perfection*.

# THE WAY OF PERFECTION

LOVE OF OTHERS

3

DETACHMENT

TRUE HUMILITY

# SOME BASIC DISPOSITIONS
# FOR A LIFE OF PRAYER

Before speaking about prayer there are some things that need to be made clear.

Being a praying person involves living in such a way as to please God, for prayer and self indulgence do not go together.

Everybody wants to preserve inward and outward peace in order to serve God in tranquillity. For this three things are necessary.

Love of others.
Detachment.
True humility.

We have to understand how important these three things are, especially humility.
And we must also have the courage necessary for a life given to God in love and service.

It isn't easy, but it is worthwhile to master the basics before trying to proceed, for one holy person is worth more than any number of mediocre ones.

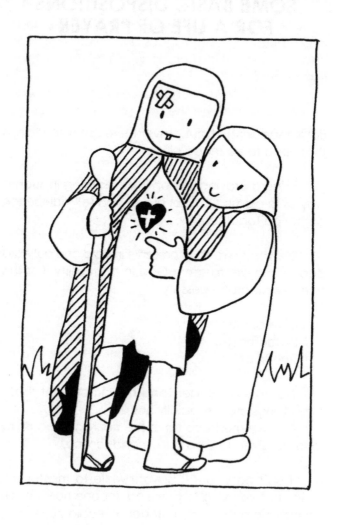

SOME BASIC DISPOSITIONS
FOR A LIFE OF PRAYER

## Love of others

To begin with, in loving those around us let us learn to get beyond appearances and love their inward beauty, even if it is often disguised by an unattractive exterior.

We need to know how to pierce the outward façade and discover the Lord who dwells in everyone's heart.

Real love doesn't change. It remains securely in place through thick and thin; whereas just loving those who naturally please us leads to dependency and slavery, for we fear the loss of their reciprocal affection. Let us love freely, without clinging or sentimentality. Above all, let us love the One who purchased us by his blood.

And don't think those who love God don't really care about others. They actually love them with a deeper, better and more genuine love, because it is a love given out of deep respect for the person, and not dependent on outward gifts.

That is real love, not the sort of counterfeit that passes for love so often but which is merely self-serving when you get down to the roots of what's happening.

Real love wants the good of the other, and resembles the love Jesus bore for us and for his Father. Real love isn't shocked by faults or put off by dis-

courtesy. Real love does not change but remains always sure and secure, for then we are loving others as God loves us.

That doesn't mean we can't have friends.

Having good friends is one way of getting to know God – that's my experience. We all need support on the journey and friends help us along.

Giving love to others makes us more generous in giving love to God. We become giving persons, outgoing, accepting, merciful, non-judgmental. And this quality makes us like the God we want to know and worship ever more deeply and truly.

## Detachment

Detachment means the freedom to love God above all, without caring unduly about the other things that so often take up our time and our energy – such as thoughts of what we own or want to own, the state of our health, our food, our leisure... all the many 'nothings' that keep us entangled in pursuits of no lasting value.

However, freedom from material things is only a first step. When it comes down to it what really matters is detaching ourselves from ourselves – and that's no easy matter. It's fine to talk about or write about, but putting it into practice is far more difficult.

What about the way we get entangled in all the business of our extended families? We can't banish them from our minds. At every opportunity we get ourselves mixed up in their business and their decisions, when this is usually a sheer waste of effort. God is perfectly able to take care of them and, in any case, they may prefer to manage their own affairs without our help! I don't count parents, brothers and sisters in this stricture. We are bound to them and they to us by ties of blood that demand our attention and care. Apart from that, let us love those God gives us as our life-companions, whoever they may be, and not meddle with the affairs of everyone who is only slightly related and who won't thank us for our busy-bodying.

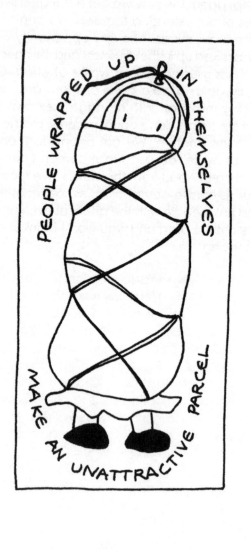

## *True humility*

Detachment from persons is one level of detachment from self. The next level is even more difficult and it is inseparable from humility.

How can we attain the freedom we need to serve God when our first concern is ourselves: our health, our self-image, our worries about what other people think of us?

As for penance... Spectacular feats of renunciation are not what count. The daily round, quietly and regularly embraced with love, yields plenty to be going on with.

Even so, we need to be careful about over-indulging ourselves. You know what the body is like – give it an inch and it takes a mile! We complain about the slightest wee pain as if we were in the throes of death itself, whereas silence would be more appropriate. Real illness is obvious and I am not talking about that here. Learn to suffer a little without broadcasting the fact to all and sundry. If we practise silence in this way we will gradually gain the mastery over ourselves and be ready to offer our whole lives to God.

But, as I've already said, it isn't the exterior thing that is the most important – the interior is what counts. Watch your thoughts as well as your actions, especially those thoughts which dwell on supposed

slights from others or which focus continually on worries about whether people are showing you sufficient respect or giving you the first place when you think it is your due. All this seeking to be first is a real barrier to progress, and it is made worse when others sympathize with us about imagined 'slights' and put-downs. We can fancy insults where none were meant and so make ourselves unhappy for no reason. How silly!

Think about the passion of Christ. Did Jesus deserve what he got? Never! And you want to be his follower only when things go your way? Forget it!

As for excusing yourself by saying 'I'm no angel' or 'I'm no saint' – too true! But that is not an excuse that holds water. You are called to holiness along with everyone else, called to be a saint. So get down to it in earnest.

# MAKING A START

Now I will proceed to talk more about prayer itself, which depends so much on the foregoing virtues if we are to make any progress at all.

For one thing, humility means being content with the kind of prayer God gives us and not insisting on the higher reaches of contemplation as if it was our 'right'. Discouragement about where you are or think you are on the road to union with God is useless. Don't give in to it but keep on doing your best and waiting for the Lord to act as he thinks fit.

For people who are fond of prayer and like their own company plenty of books have been written. Such books describe the life of our Lord in short passages or treat of other good subjects in manageable portions. This helps to give prayer time a structure and holds the thoughts on God. People who can use books like these are on a straight road that will eventually lead them to their goal. They walk restfully and securely, because one cannot help but be at peace when the understanding is harnessed to good subjects and is engrossed in matters relating to God.

Others just say vocal prayers with attention. This too is admirable.

Others alas have such butterfly minds that when they try to fix their thoughts on God they are assailed by a thousand foolish ideas; their thoughts run hither and thither and it is impossible to control them (or so it seems). People can either be born this way or become so in the course of their life. Prayer for them is a continual struggle.

If you are like these people then the advice I give is that on no account should you give up. Every journey begins with a single step – take it. One step will take you nearer to God, and even if you do not progress further at least you have made a good start and cannot possibly come to harm.

MARTHA

MARY

St Martha was holy but from the Gospels it doesn't seem that she would count as a 'contemplative' in the usual sense of that word. But she was certainly a dear friend of Jesus and was chosen to serve him faithfully and lovingly. So if your way to God is through service why complain? Someone has to cook the meals! We can't all sit around like Mary. Society needs all sorts to keep going. Contemplation, mental prayer, tending the sick, preparing the food... Everything combines to greet the Guest who comes to us in one way or another. Don't be choosy about your tasks. Do what is necessary and what seems to be your personal calling without comparing yourself with others or fussing about the degree of 'contemplation' you have or have not reached. That is a waste of time!

Those God calls to the highest reaches of prayer are always courageous in undergoing suffering and are humble enough to accept whatever God chooses to give them.

## A Simile

Prayer can be likened to water. It is something we long for when we don't have it. And this water has been promised to us by Jesus himself, so we can be sure of getting it if we ask in faith.

Water has three properties among many others: it cools, it cleans, and it quenches thirst.

God is ever ready to give the water of prayer that it might be all these things to us.

Go on then to reach this water that all your longings may be satisfied. God invites you but does not force you to drink unless you wish to do so. He will always respect your free will.

If you do decide to seek this water, God will also make sure that there is enough provided en route to enable you to persevere in your quest without dying of thirst. There are many streams, large and small, flowing from the one source. Don't fear that you will have nothing to sustain you along the way.

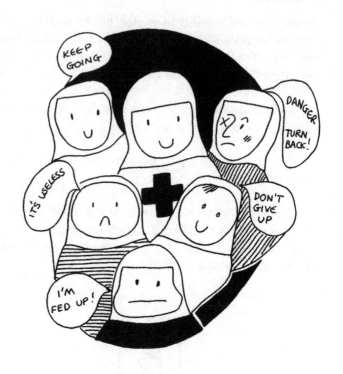

## The importance of resolution

Beginnings are important. That isn't to say that every part of the journey isn't important, but the beginning sets the tone of the whole enterprise. So set out with an earnest and 'determined determination' to reach the fountain of living water promised by Jesus.

Resolve not to stop until you reach your goal, no matter what comes, no matter what happens, no matter how hard you have to labour, no matter what other people may say to deter you. There will be plenty of folk who try to make you turn back with all sorts of tales about others who went astray on the road of prayer. Pay no attention to their tales of woe. The treasure is worthy of any risk.

Some people like to take life peaceably, but when it comes to gaining some material benefit such as an increase of wealth how they work! And what's more, they think nothing of all the effort they put into obtaining a miserable increase in salary.

Take my advice – go for true riches. Prayer is the road that takes you to the fountain of life and happiness. If anyone tries to tell you another road will do just as well don't believe them. Only believe people who model their lives on Christ. One Christlike person who sees and speaks the truth can make a real difference, and will be able to encourage you when things seem hopeless.

To conclude, keep these three maxims in mind:

1. Try to have a good conscience,
2. Despise worldly values,
3. Believe firmly in the teaching of the Church.

Then stop worrying! Go right ahead!

# VOCAL AND MENTAL PRAYER

Mental prayer has nothing to do with keeping the lips closed.

If I speak to God, consciously remembering I am in God's presence and thinking of the words I am saying, then I am praying mentally with mind and voice as one.

When you pray, think of the One you are addressing and think of who you yourself are. Don't take a merely casual approach. Use your minds! Couples who are in love want to know all they can about each other. If you love Jesus, then try to discover more about him. Don't speak to him when thinking about other things as if this didn't matter. Understand Jesus. Understand yourself.

Give God the time you have decided to give without reservation. Don't be like someone who offers a friend a gift and then tries to take it back. That's barefaced meanness. Time devoted to God is meant to be for God alone. Keep that intention firm.

Another reason to be firm is that a resolute person fights with greater fierceness, knowing that they must not retreat – like an army standard bearer who, if he runs from the field, will be killed later anyway. His life depends upon gaining the victory.

If we fight with the same determination we shall get what we want in the end. In fact we think it will be hard when actually we experience joy and the gift of friendship along the way. God is good. Once we taste this goodness we find the courage to keep going, realizing that Jesus has actually paid the price for us anyway. Even in this life we receive a hundredfold. We ask and are given what we ask for as Jesus promised.

CONVERSATION BETWEEN FRIENDS ·····

Now, coming back to those poor people I mentioned who find it hard to concentrate when they pray. The first thing to do is to learn to say your prayers well. Don't try and enter into all kinds of convoluted reasoning which tires you out. It isn't your fault if you don't seem able to get close to God.

And don't suppose that just because you cannot hear God speaking to you God is actually silent. He speaks clearly to our heart when from our heart we beg him to do so. He is never far away. Just try and stay with him in whatever way you can.

Some impatient people don't like taking any trouble, and it certainly does take time and patience to get into the habit of prayer.

I have found the most helpful thing is to try and companion Jesus so as to pray more attentively. In fact, by speaking to him, even if only by saying prayers, we can reach the heights of contemplation and be filled with joy and peace.

Of course we can't reach that state just by our own efforts, but we must do whatever we can do and trust God to make up the shortfall.

## *Vocal prayer*

When beginning to pray vocally start with:
1. an examination of conscience
2. confession of sin
3. the sign of the cross

CONFESSION OF SIN · SIGN OF THE CROSS · EXAMINATION OF CONSCIENCE

PREPARING FOR PRAYER

Then, as you are alone, look for a companion to teach you how to pray and what to say. For that there could be no better person than our Lord himself and the prayer he taught us, the Our Father.

Imagine that he is at your side, and notice how lovingly and humbly he is teaching you.

If you accustom yourself to being with him, and try to please him, you will never be able to send him away, nor will he ever fail you.

To those whose minds are constantly wandering I say – form this habit. It is possible as I know from experience – so persevere. I am not suggesting long or complicated thoughts about Jesus, only that you should look at him as he looks at you; and with him beside you, say the prayer he taught us.

If you want Jesus you can have him. He is just longing for your look of love, so don't disappoint him!

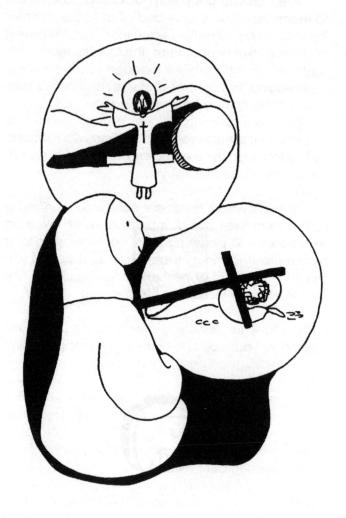

There are as many ways to look at him as you have moods:

If you are happy, look upon Jesus risen – his brightness and beauty will gladden your heart and increase your joy.

If you are suffering look on Jesus as he goes to Gethsemane, or bound to the column of scourging, spat upon, denied by his friends, cold and alone. Offer him comfort.

Or look upon Jesus bent double under the weight of the cross. Allow him to gaze at you then with his eyes full of compassionate tears as you bear him company. You will then realize the value of suffering and the reality of the pain that the Lord bore for you, which is so much greater than anything you will be asked to bear for him.

Or try putting yourself in the place of Mary Magdalen or the Blessed Virgin. Let them guide your thoughts as you strive to be present on Calvary.

Another help is to find a picture of Jesus that appeals to you and look at it regularly when you are at prayer. This will make the Lord more real to you.

And don't say that all this is too complicated and difficult. You aren't short of words to talk to people around you, so there's no reason to run out of things to say when you talk to God and know he is present with you.

Just keep at the side of the Master, Jesus, and resolve to learn all he wants to teach you. He will never leave you unless you leave him first.

Consider his words, his deeds, and be convinced of his love. Use your imagination – your heart as well as your head.

Let the Lord's own prayer be your model when you begin to pray. That way you cannot go wrong.

# OUR FATHER

## *Learning about the Father through his Son*

Here at the very beginning of this prayer, I see God the Father revealed as the Father of such a wonderful Son. O how appropriate then it is for me to rise above myself so that the Son might reveal the Father to me.

And yet I am about to pray with Jesus as my very brother.

The Jesus who has taken our nature and come to live among us. What a great mystery!

With all this to ponder would it be right to stop trying to think of Jesus lest the thought of such love tear our heart to pieces? Of course not!

Another point is that we are all children of this one Father, regardless of how high or low our family tree takes us on the ladder of society. Jesus overturns all these niceties by choosing all sorts to be his disciples, and all on the same level of equality.

Our thoughts, dwelling on the mystery of the Father and the Son must perforce be enkindled by the presence of the Holy Spirit. May that same Spirit light the fire of love in our own hearts.

# WHO ART IN HEAVEN

## *Heaven is within us*

You know that God is everywhere and however quietly we may speak he hears us. There is no need for wings to go in search of him. We can talk to him with absolute trust and familiarity, not keeping our distance out of a wrong sort of 'respect'.

The Lord of Heaven is actually within us, and if we enter within ourselves we find ourselves with God. He is there just as he was present in the womb of the Virgin Mary. And as he loves us, he makes us, as he did her, with an interior space capable of receiving him.

Those who find God within don't have to make long journeys. They quickly reach their goal. The soul seems to gather itself up into itself, its eyes close – at first with effort, but soon quite naturally, and it attains peace and tranquillity.

This is recollection. It is as if such people have set out on the seas and skim along fanned by the fires of love.

Attention to God quickly becomes second nature once the effort is made. God asks only for our interior space to be given, and for us to allow him to put in or take out whatever he pleases. If we give ourselves wholly to God, God repays our generosity swiftly with the gift of himself.

Check temptation in all its guises by remembering that what the kingdom God offers is not a kingdom of this world. What does the praise of people matter if we are intent only on pleasing God?

The kind of contemplation I am talking about at this point is one we can attain by our own effort, aided as always by God's grace.

Keep your senses occupied by good thoughts, bring the imagination into play.

Say the Our Father with attention and you will speedily find yourself in the habit and making great progress. Time spent in this manner is never wasted.

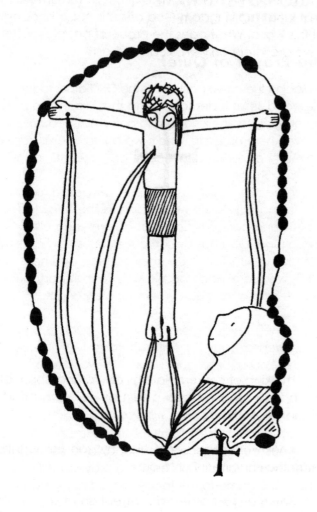

## HALLOWED BE THY NAME
## THY KINGDOM COME

### *The Prayer of Quiet*

In placing these two petitions of the Our Father together, the good Jesus is demonstrating that we should pray unceasingly for the kingdom to be established among us even here on earth. And if we ask for the kingdom we must be prepared to receive it by doing God's will.

In heaven, real joy is in the perpetual peace and tranquillity of the soul, and in the knowledge that its one concern and that of everyone else is in loving God. God has become the soul's new centre. In knowing him, love becomes perfect; and here on earth we are already on the way to that perfection of love and knowledge when we pray aright.

Sometimes during prayer the Lord grants us a taste of heaven already, allowing us to rest in quietness, teaching our understanding in ways beyond our grasp.

People can be raised to the prayer of quiet through saying their vocal prayers well. Someone I know used to say a number of paternosters corresponding to the times our Lord shed his blood, and she would spend two or three hours on these prayers and a few others. She came to me to say she did not know how to practise mental prayer, but when I questioned her I realised that she was experiencing pure contemplation, the gift of union. And she was proving this by her

actions. This example shows that vocal prayer well said is sufficient to make us contemplative.

Now I want to say a bit more about this prayer of quiet, when God begins to give us his kingdom here on earth so that we can truly praise and hallow his name.

The prayer of quiet is a supernatural state that cannot be obtained simply by our trying hard to reach it. It is a state when the soul enters into peace, being offered the gift of peace through God's presence. Without being aware of it in the senses, the soul realizes that it is now very close to God, and if it were just a little closer it would become one through union.

This is demonstrated by the story of the just man Simeon who was able to see beneath appearances and accept the tiny baby presented in the temple as the promised Messiah. Outwardly the infant was only the child of two poor people; but then he revealed himself to the old man for who and what he really was, the Son of the Father. In the same way, the soul dimly recognises and knows the presence of Christ, even though it does not understand how that comes about. Without asking for anything it intu-its its closeness to the King and the kingdom, and this joy also affects the body.

In this state the faculties are stilled. Mind and memory no longer work. All is taken up into God in deep absorption.

Occasionally the prayer of quiet will last several days and has the effect of overflowing into the actions of the person concerned. It seems to them that their will (or power of love and choice) is taken over by God even while they busy themselves outwardly with other duties.

In this state Martha and Mary are really working in unison. The will remains absorbed in contemplation even while mind and memory carry on with ordinary tasks.

This state can be the cause of tears shed in deep joy, and there is a longing to remain with the Lord as the disciples longed to remain on Tabor. However, like the disciples, this joy cannot be prolonged indefinitely, still less can it be made to stay by trying to curtail movement, hold the breath, or do other foolish things. This gift is pure gift and not within our control, any more than daybreak or nightfall respond to our whim. All we can do is put no obstacle in the way and seek solitude if that is possible, so that we give the Lord maximum opportunity to work within us.

If the mind continues to wander when we are in this state take no notice at all. Remain like a child at the breast of God. God gives it milk without having to be asked. Just so the will in this state simply loves, and is not meant to understand how or why this happens. If the understanding is taxed the mind will lapse into a quandary and the soul lose the Divine sustenance it was receiving.

This is still not union; for in union God places nourishment in the soul without the soul even having to nurse at the breast. As things are the soul must still work a little to extract the milk, though it does so very quietly and barely conscious of doing anything.

The happiness attendant on this state is such that all the wealth and possessions that the world can offer are as nothing compared with the inward satisfaction the soul feels in its depths, even though various unruly thoughts may still plague it.

In this state of prayer the Father seems to have given the soul the kingdom already here on earth. Yet when God grants this favour we have to realize that we have not yet reached the end of the journey. It is not a gift given so that we can become proud, but more humble. We certainly should not throw the gift back in God's face by living carelessly.

In my experience many come thus far in prayer but few go further. They do not respond to the graces offered and just go on talking to God as in times past instead of remaining silently before him.

If this favour is granted to you, be watchful. Don't lose the treasure through carelessness.

## THY WILL BE DONE ON EARTH
## AS IT IS IN HEAVEN

### *Total self-offering*

The Lord has not only asked us to make this request of the Father but has given us the example we need to put it into practice. What we have to do is place ourselves freely in his hands that he may do as he will with us.

Good words are not sufficient of themselves. We have to make such sentiments practical and effective in our lives.

It amuses me for sure when some seem to think that trials depend on our asking God for them. They come to everyone anyway. And whether we wish it or not God's will must be done in heaven and on earth, so believe me and make a virtue of necessity!

Do you want to see how the Father treats those who give themselves wholly to him? Look at his Son and you will see. Think how sincerely Jesus prayed in the garden of Gesthemane. Think of all he endured in the way of suffering until at last his life ended on the cross.

When you see how God treated his best Beloved, you will realize that a mark of God's love is the suffering he asks us to bear. Those who love God a lot are able to bear much suffering, those who

71

love God only a little can bear only a little. And thus God gives according to the courage he sees in us.

We just have to place ourselves completely in God's hands. And the more resolutely we do this, accepting all that God sends us, all that God asks of us, the more God will draw us to himself and the more we will experience the joy that comes from total self-giving.

So don't restrict your prayers to words alone. Give God the jewel of your total self-offering. And don't be like those who proffer a gift and then take it back again. Give, and let go.

What I want to make clear is that we have to surrender our wills to the Creator and detach ourselves from all else. Unless we do this how can we drink of the living water he so generously provides?

If we do God's will, he in turn will do our will when we pray. And don't think you can reach this point just by your own efforts – you can't. Be simple. Be humble. Simplicity and humility achieve all, and allow God to fulfil his will completely in our lives.

# GIVE US THIS DAY OUR DAILY BREAD

## *The gift of the Eucharist*

We need Jesus every day. Without him we do not have the necessary means to do the Father's will. He has remained with us in the Blessed Sacrament for this purpose, and in this Sacrament the Son is present with us until the end of the world, offering himself continually to the Father on our behalf.

This daily gift of Jesus to us, a gift that is ours in Holy Communion, is given to sustain us in doing the Father's will. It is a bread we need far more than we need earthly nourishment.

God will provide all else that is necessary in the way of material things, so do not be anxious. Seek his kingdom first. Don't be like a servant begging his master to feed him. That is a waste of words. God, like a good householder, will provide for his whole family without having to be asked. In fact you will find the Blessed Sacrament a remedy even for physical ills.

Just as Jesus walked among people on earth, healing and blessing, so he does today. No need to regret not having been born during his earthly life, not having seen him with your bodily eyes. In faith we know he is just as present here and now as he was then – in fact, even closer. Healings took place when people touched him, but in Communion he is actually within you.

After Communion place yourself before Jesus like the Magdalen. Anoint him and weep for your sins. Or consider the scenes of the Passion and know he is truly there as he was on the cross. Spend the time after Communion in intimate conversation with the Guest of your soul. Allow him to teach you all he wants.

Usually I like seeing pictures of the Lord around me, but at the time of Communion these are super-fluous. Remain with Christ for as long as possible and then take him with you to all the daily tasks that await you outside the Church.

Try always to receive Jesus with the proper dispositions. Remember that in many places the Blessed Sacrament is not loved and honoured as it should be. We cannot make up for this by ourselves, but the Father has given us his only Son to do all that we cannot do. How blessed are we, how blessed the whole Church in this wonderful gift!

# FORGIVE US OUR TRESSPASSES AS WE FORGIVE THOSE WHO TRESSPASS AGAINST US

## *Becoming like God in merciful love*

Our good Master sees that if we have the heavenly food of Communion we are required to forgive those who are indebted to us. Indeed, just to make this request means that in intention we must have already done so. Notice, after all, that he does not say 'As we shall forgive'.

It is a serious obligation on us to forgive others when we ourselves have been given and forgiven so much. What a scandal then if we should withhold forgiveness from anyone – especially for some imagined slights or offence to our honour.

Good gracious! How often I used to feel slighted over mere nothings! Better to forget these niceties altogether and let others look after my so-called 'honour'. How ridiculous to stand on our dignity when we have to approach God with empty hands anyway, begging for forgiveness and mercy.

Love is all 'for giving'. Jesus doesn't have us ask forgiveness because we are praying or fasting or doing penance or have left everything for him. He has us ask forgiveness because we are forgiving others. And how hard that is to poor human nature!

Yet, how can we expect mercy if we are unmerciful to those around us.

When God's grace is really at work in the soul it cares nothing about human esteem. It realizes that what people think is passing away with the breezes of fashion. The only lasting treasure is love.

Those who love like this never mind when other people know of their sins and mistakes. They don't try to cover up the truth as if they were ashamed of their humanity and need for God.

Fortitude under provocation is a mark of God's love being present within us. As a virtue, fortitude doesn't take root in a trice. But once we realize how much we have been forgiven, and how God has shown us such great mercy time and time again, we are strengthened. We then become only too happy to show mercy to others in our turn. And how this gladdens the heart of our merciful God.

So let us be open and sincere, not saying one thing and meaning another, but forgiving as we have been forgiven.

# AND LEAD US NOT INTO TEMPTATION

## *Trust in God's mercy*

Believe me, those who practice prayer and contemplation are always ready for the hour of conflict. They never turn back from the battle but go from strength to strength. Yet even so, we can be easily deceived by evil which presents itself to us under the guise of good.

One way this is done is by making people believe that the favours they experience in prayer come from God when in fact they come from the evil one. They become proud for nothing. So do not seek any extraordinary experiences or visions. Remain humble and don't give way to pride, believing that you are holy when in fact you are far from it.

Remember too that what the Lord gives he is free to take away. We can never therefore rely on good feelings. Feelings come and go. If we are feeling in good spirits we can take all sorts of difficulties in our stride. If we are feeling low the slightest contradiction puts us even more out of sorts.

So don't feel secure in being a patient person, or a prayerful person, or a person who conquers temptation. Just wait until you are put to the test and see how you manage your O-so-patient self! Doubt your own virtue or you are sure to have a heavy fall.

Another thing to be aware of is the problem of false humility. That includes a temptation to think that your past sins are unforgivable, that God is not merciful, or cannot be merciful to someone such as yourself. Real humility does not have this effect at all. It is accompanied by joy, peace and tranquillity even when you recognize your failures and sins. If you think the other kind of thing is humility then you

are mistaken. Turn your thoughts from your own wretchedness and think about God's mercy and love instead.

End every period of prayer by spending some time in self examination. That way you will not be deceived about 'favours'. Rather you will receive light on your unworthiness and God's goodness.

But don't be the kind of person who walks always in fear. Let love quicken your steps.

Those who really love God
love all good,
seek all good,
help forward all good,
and invariably join forces with other good
  people to help and defend them.

They love only truth and things that are worthy of love. They are ready to give their lives in order to find ways to please and serve God better.

And their love is evident to all for it is a love that is put into action, growing stronger by degrees all the time.

Loving God, we can be quite certain that God loves us too and will reward our efforts with eternal life in his presence.

Of course, this love must be nurtured by keeping away from sin. As we advance we will become more and more sensitive to what displeases God until we avoid it completely. Be ready to die a thousand deaths rather than cause God pain. Don't get into bad habits and think that because something isn't seriously wrong it can be treated lightly. It can't. The God of all purity loves single hearts, not divided ones.

However, don't be a sin-scrupulous person full of seriousness and self-importance, having a 'holier-than-thou' mien. Be sociable, be happy, a good and loving companion to all; otherwise you will put people off God instead of attracting them to goodness.

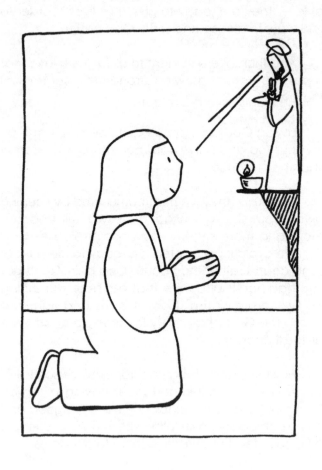

# BUT DELIVER US FROM EVIL. AMEN

## *Living in the truth*

We will always need to beg the Lord's help.

He wants us to desire truth – yet we often desire falsehood instead.

He wants us to desire what is eternal, whereas we prefer what is passing away.

He wants us to desire great and sublime things, yet we desire what is base.

He wants us to desire only what is certain, yet we desire what is of doubtful merit.

May God deliver us from living in illusion and make us live in the truth – the truth of our destiny and the truth of his love and mercy.

# CONCLUSION

So you see that everything is contained in the Lord's prayer. However many books may be taken from you, this one can never be taken away. It is Jesus' own gift, received from the lips of Truth himself.

As you repeat the Our Father daily, do so with sincerity and understanding. That way you will speedily attain to contemplation.